Pronounced "Chet"
Written in English as "Ch"

Practice writing ten (10) times

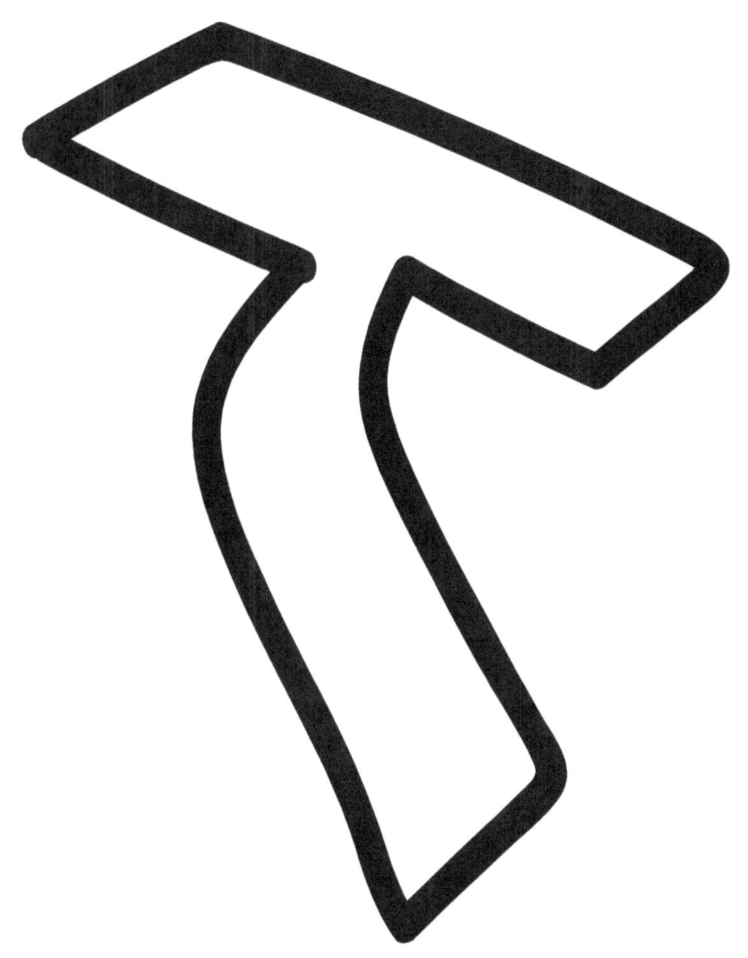

Pronounced "Zayin"
Written in English as "Z"

Practice writing ten (10) times

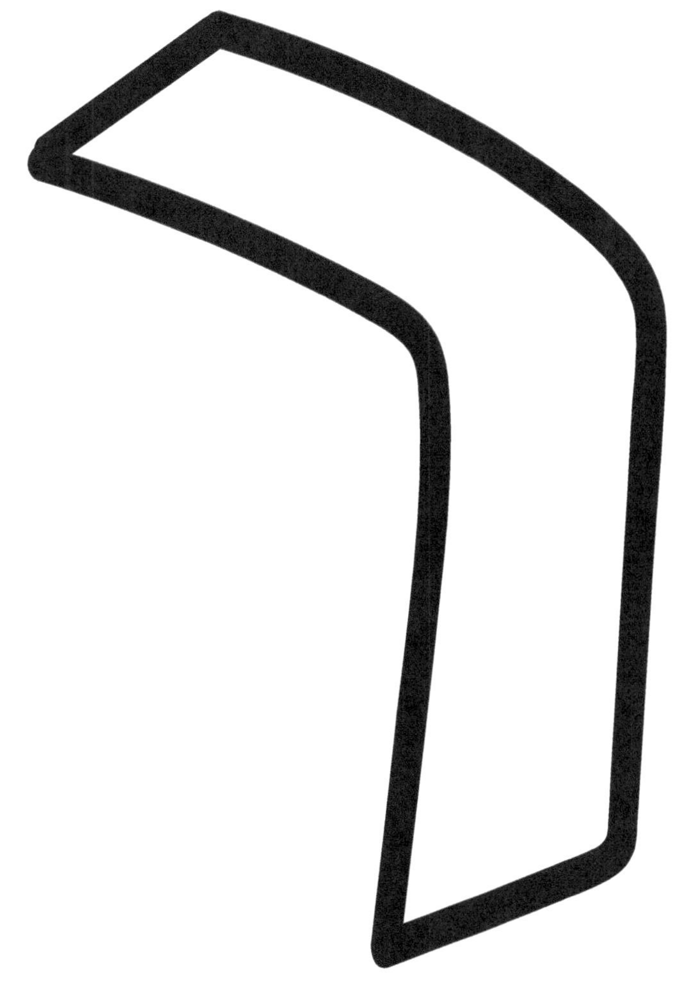

Pronounced "Vav"
Written in English as "V"

Practice writing ten (10) times

<table>
<tr><td></td><td></td><td></td><td></td><td></td><td></td><td></td><td></td><td></td><td></td></tr>
</table>

Pronounced "He"
Written in English as "H"

Practice writing ten (10) times

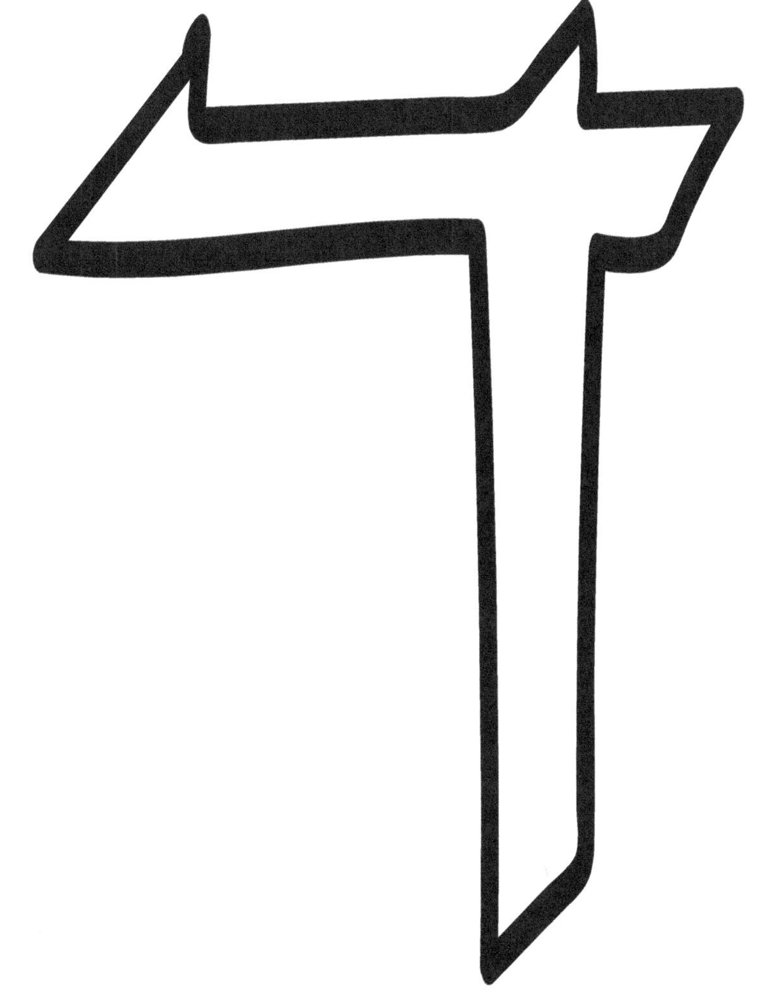

Pronounced "Dalet"
Written in English as "D"

Practice writing ten (10) times

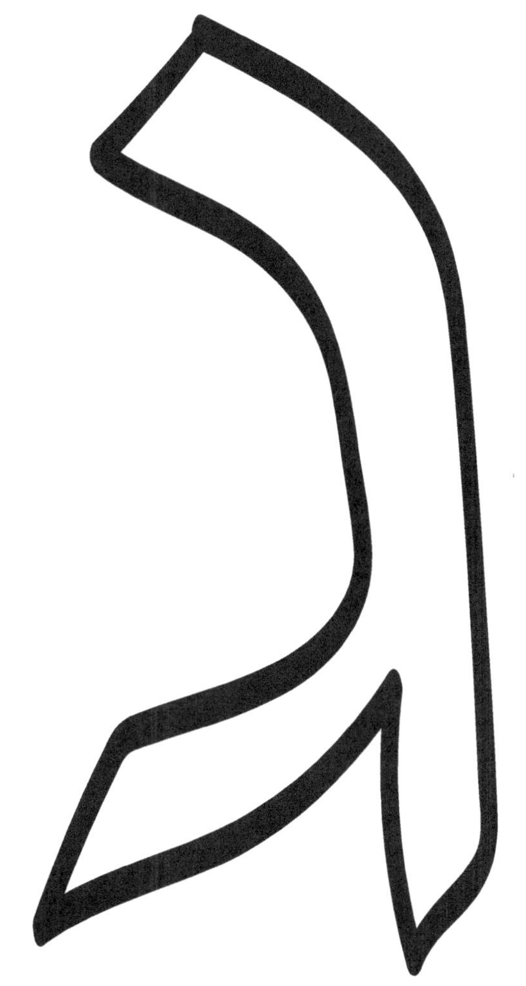

Pronounced "Gimel"
Written in English as "G"

Practice writing ten (10) times

Pronounced "Bet"
Written in English as "B" or "V"

Practice writing ten (10) times

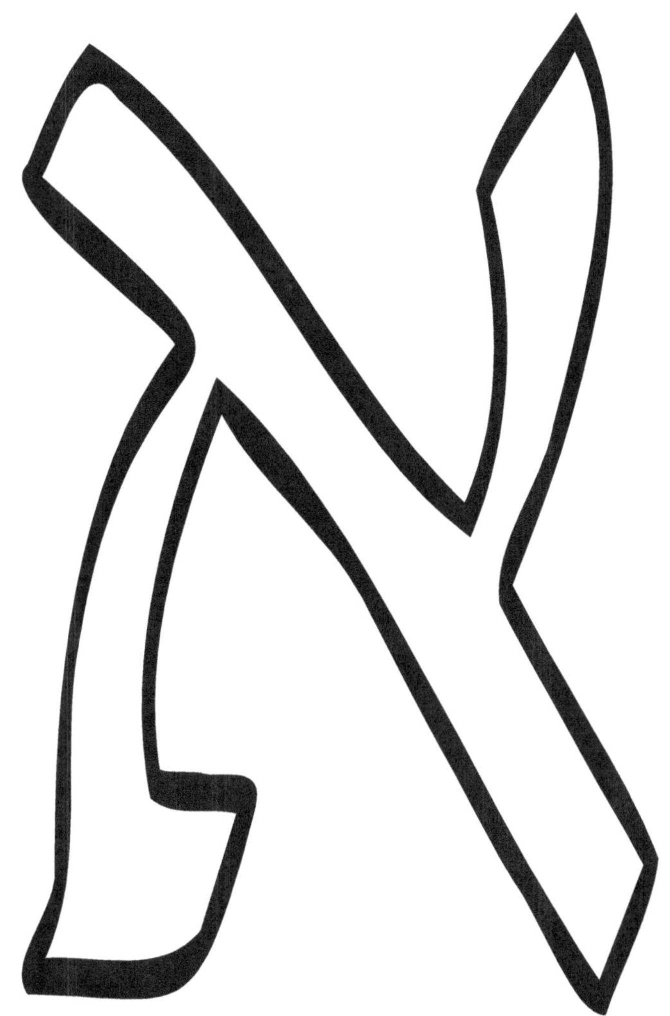

Pronounced "Alef"
Written in English as "silent"

Practice writing ten (10) times

Pronounced "Ayin"
Written in English as "silent"

Practice writing ten (10) times

<table>
<tr><td> </td><td> </td><td> </td><td> </td><td> </td><td> </td><td> </td><td> </td><td> </td><td> </td></tr>
</table>

Pronounced "Samech"
Written in English as "S"

Practice writing ten (10) times

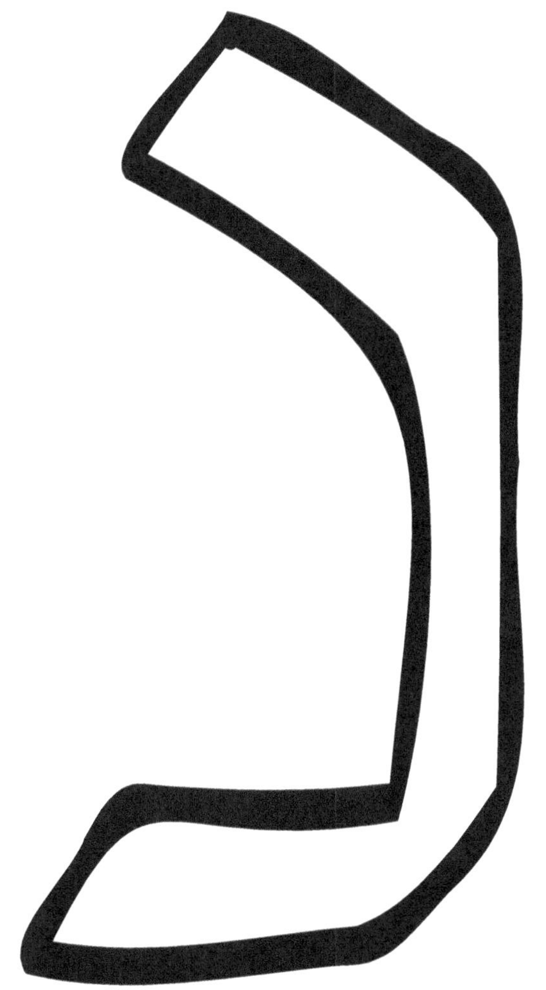

Pronounced "Nun"
Written in English as "N"

Practice writing ten (10) times

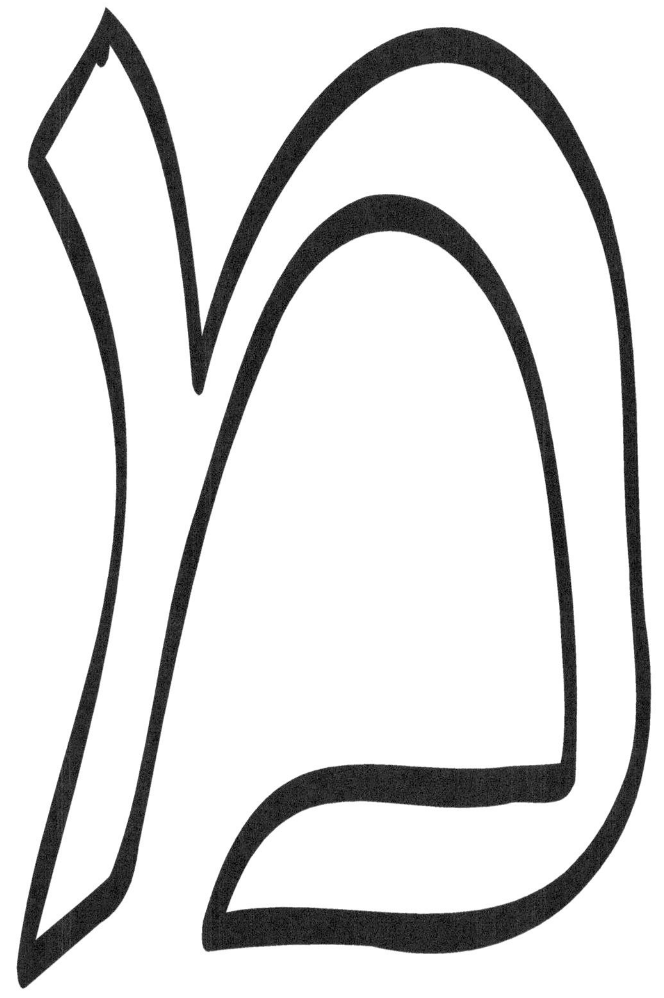

Pronounced "Mem"
Written in English as "M"

Practice writing ten (10) times

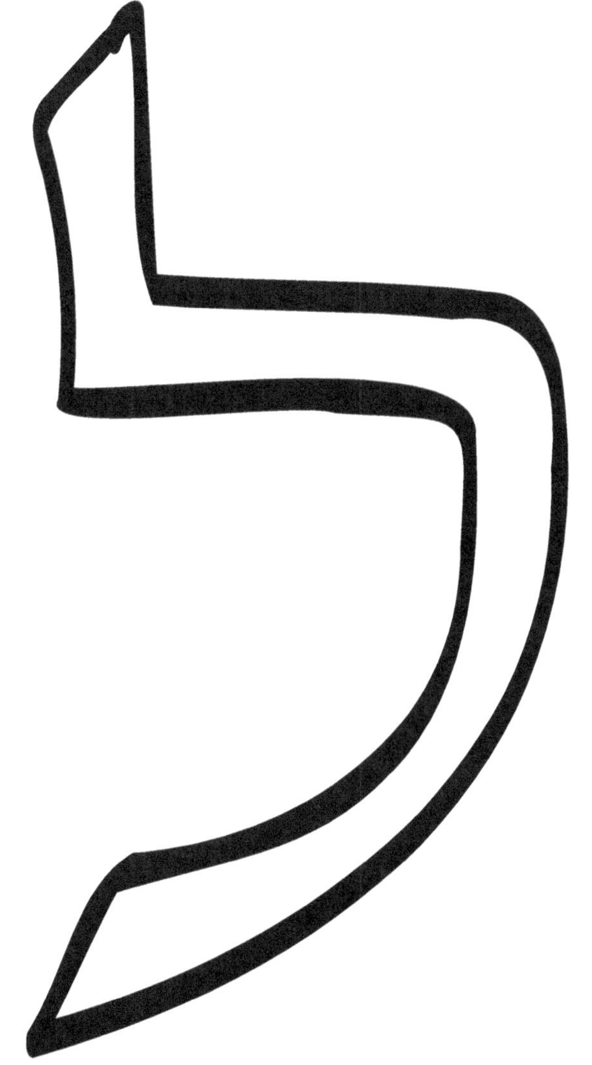

Pronounced "Lamed"
Written in English as "L"

Practice writing ten (10) times

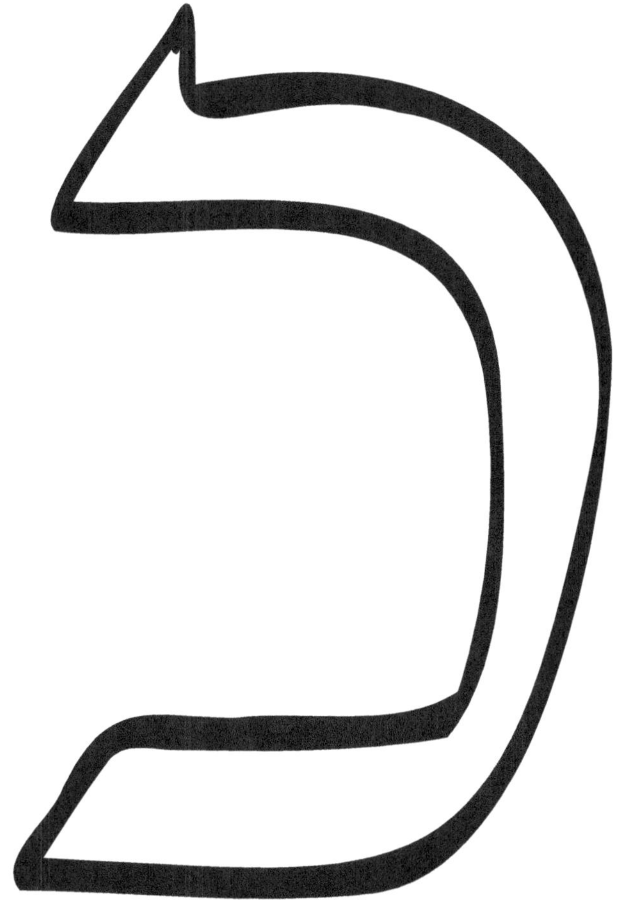

Pronounced "Kaf"
Written in English as "K" or "Kh"

Practice writing ten (10) times

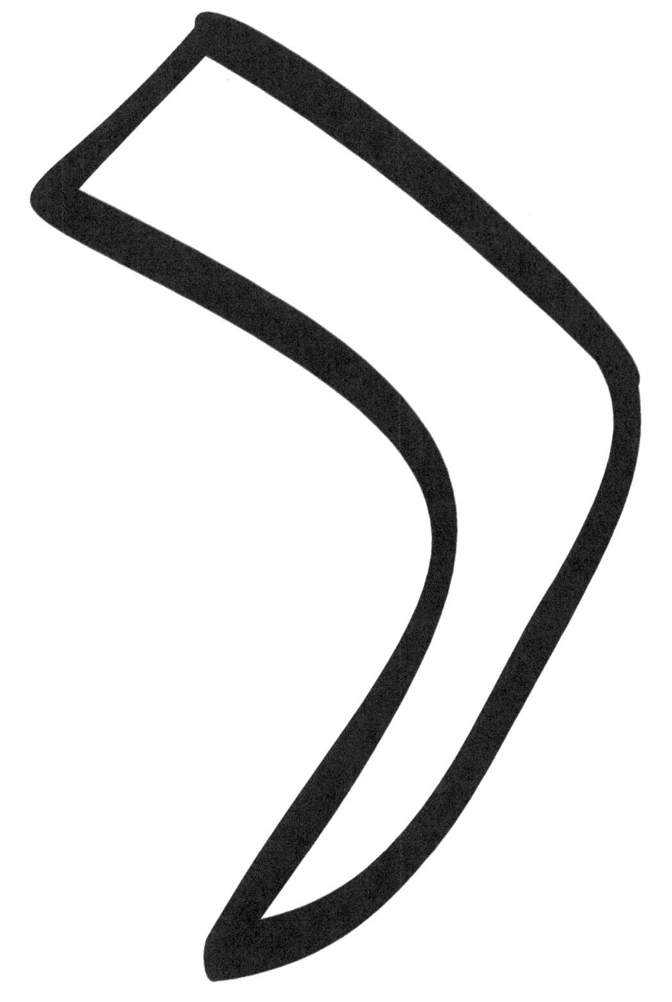

Pronounced "Yod"
Written in English as "Y"

Practice writing ten (10) times

Pronounced "Tet"
Written in English as "T"

Practice writing ten (10) times

<table>
<tr><td></td><td></td><td></td><td></td><td></td><td></td><td></td><td></td><td></td><td></td></tr>
</table>

Pronounced "Tav"
Written in English as "T"

Practice writing ten (10) times

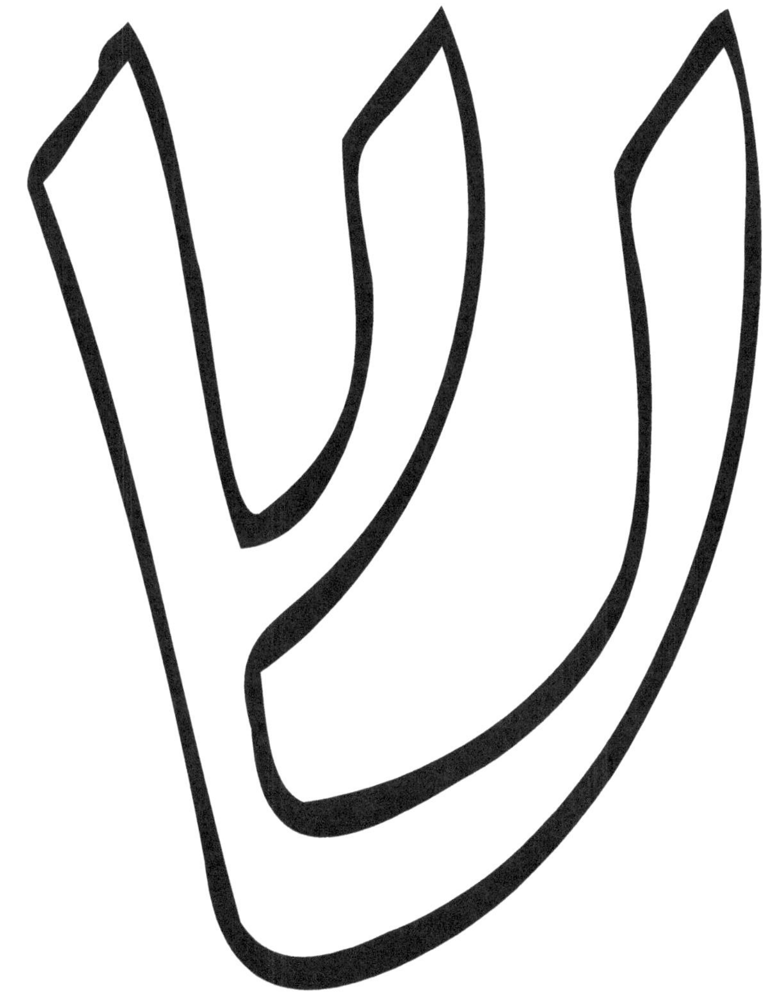

Pronounced "Shin"
Written in English as "Sh" or "S"

Practice writing ten (10) times

<table>
<tr><td> </td><td> </td><td> </td><td> </td><td> </td><td> </td><td> </td><td> </td><td> </td><td> </td></tr>
</table>

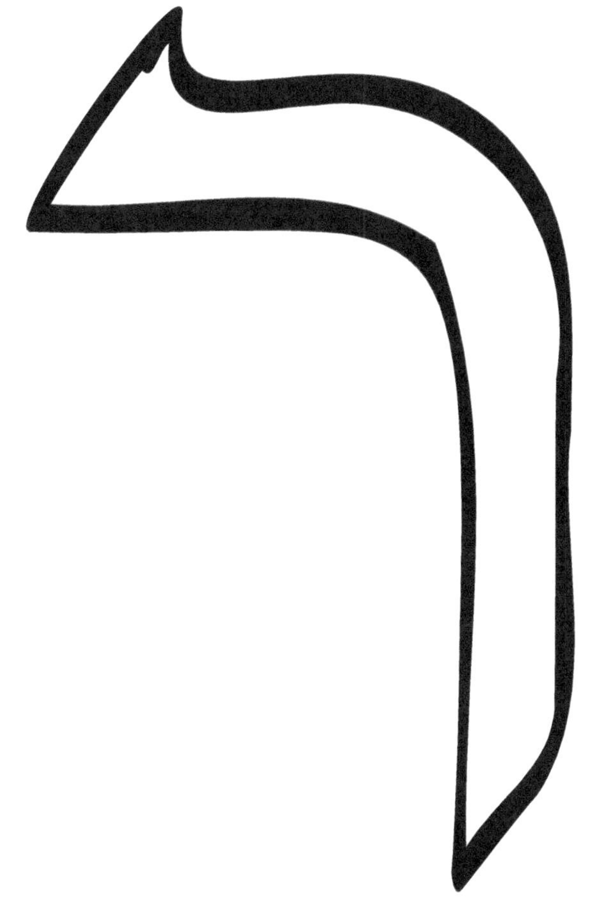

Pronounced "Resh"
Written in English as "R"

Practice writing ten (10) times

Pronounced "Qof"
Written in English as "Q"

Practice writing ten (10) times

<table>
<tr><td></td><td></td><td></td><td></td><td></td><td></td><td></td><td></td><td></td><td></td></tr>
</table>

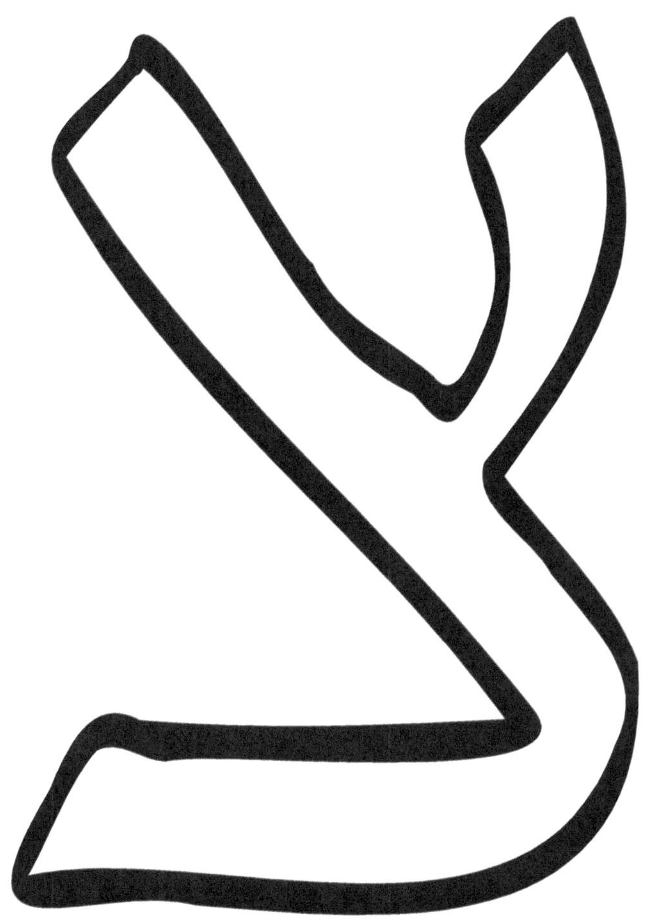

Pronounced "Tsadeh"
Written in English as "Ts"

Practice writing ten (10) times

<table>
<tr><td></td><td></td><td></td><td></td><td></td><td></td><td></td><td></td><td></td><td></td></tr>
</table>

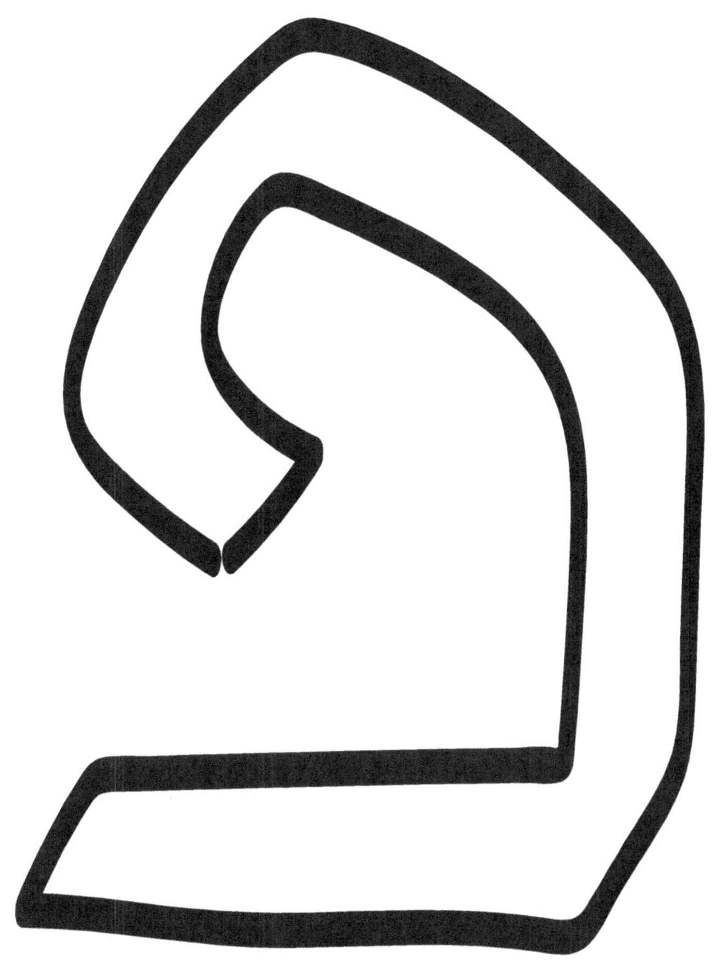

Pronounced "Peh"
Written in English as "P" or "F"

Practice writing ten (10) times
